Cliff Diving

by Ellen Labrecque

Published by The Child's World®
1980 Lookout Drive
Mankato, MN 56003-1705
800-599-READ
www.childsworld.com

The Child's World®: Mary Berendes, Publishing Director
Shoreline Publishing Group, LLC: James Buckley Jr.,
    Production Director
The Design Lab: Design and production

ISBN 9781609731786
LCCN 2011940081

Photo credits: Cover: iStock.
Interior: AP/Wide World: 4, 12, 15, 16, 19, 20, 23, 24;
Corbis: 27; Courtesy Sheraton Maui: 7; dreamstime.
com: Steve Allen: 8, Steve Heap: 28;

Printed in the United States of America

Table of Contents

Orlando Duque is one of the world's best cliff divers.

CHAPTER ONE

Jump Off a Cliff!

Orlando "The Duke" Duque stands at the top of a cliff. The cliff towers 85 feet (26 m) above the surface of the water! Imagine standing atop an eight-story building! The Duke wears only his bathing suit. He takes a deep breath and leaps off the cliff. He does somersaults and twists in the air. In just three seconds, he lands feet first in the water below.

He enters the water falling as fast as a car drives on a highway (62 miles per hour). But the diver barely makes a splash. The crowd watching from above waits nervously. Then Duque's head pops back up. He made it! Now, he just has to battle rough waves to reach the bottom of the cliff. He climbs on the jagged rocks to get back on land—safe and sound.

Welcome to the terrifying, heart-stopping sport of cliff diving!

From cliffs and bluffs above the ocean, brave men and women show their skills and bravery. Cliff diving takes nerves of steel and years of training.

The sport itself is hundreds of years old. In 1770, King Kahekili, of Maui, Hawaii, dove off a 63-foot (19-m) cliff. For his high-flying jumps, the king earned the nickname "Birdman" from visiting English sailors. He also became famous for the words "lele kawa." In English, those Hawaiian words mean "jumping off high cliffs and entering the water feet first without a splash." The king's warriors wanted to prove their bravery to their king. They soon performed lele kawa too. The sport of cliff diving was born.

A hotel in Hawaii celebrates the king's ancient dive with a nightly ceremony.

Tourists in boats get a great view of the Acapulco cliff divers.

For close to 200 years, cliff diving was only popular with very small groups of people. Then in the 1930s, cliff diving became more well-known because of a famous spot in Acapulco, Mexico. A diving club there began in 1934, when young boys jumped 95 feet (29 m) off the cliffs of La Quebrada (la kay-BRAH-dah; or in English, the gorge). The boys performed the jumps for **tourists** in the hopes of earning a few **pesos**. Timing is **crucial** for the La Quebrada divers. The depth of the water can be as shallow as six feet (2 m), or as deep as 16 feet (5 m), depending upon the waves. Deeper water, of course, is safer for the diver.

Perfect Timing

People gather all around the **cove** in Acapulco where cliff divers perform. The divers make their jumps every day at 1 pm. They must time their jumps just right. They need to enter the water when it is highest. If they dive too soon—or too late—the water below might be dangerously shallow! Still, these expert divers rarely have accidents.

In the 1950s, a watch company called Timex brought the Acapulco cliff divers to worldwide attention. Timex filmed a commercial of a cliff diver wearing one of its watches as he dove from the heights of La Quebrada. After the dive, the diver climbed out of the water and showed off his watch. The announcer said, "Timex takes a licking, but keeps on ticking." Since then, cliff diving has spread around the world. Daring divers leap from spots around the world. But they always look—and train—before they leap.

Divers in Mexico have to jump out from the cliff before they plunge toward the water.

A diver prepares carefully before making a jump.

CHAPTER TWO

Cliffs Are for the Brave

What does it take to be a cliff diver? They have to be fit and very flexible. They must also be strong swimmers. Most importantly, they have to be brave! They need guts and nerve to leap off **colossal** cliffs. Cliff divers have to be fearless.

Most cliff divers say the hardest part of their dive is right before they leap off the cliff. Doubt and fear can enter a diver's mind. They must stay strong mentally. Many divers count to 10 before they make the leap. This helps calm their nerves.

"The physical part is always there," says Orlando Duque, who is a nine-time world cliff diving champion. "You are strong if you did the training. But you have to deal with the mental part of the dive as well."

Dives of the World
Along with Acapulco, the most famous cliff diving spots are in Hawaii, Jamaica, Australia, and Switzerland. Hawaii has wonderful weather and high volcano cliff banks. Australia's cliffs loom over rivers and lakes instead of oceans. Cliffs over the Ord River in Western Australia are 84 feet (25.6 m) high. In the tiny village of Brontallo, Switzerland, divers leap off Alpine hills into the beautiful, clear Maggia River.

After a careful check of the landing area, the diver steps to the edge of the cliff. He bends his knees a few times, gets his balance . . . and then with a powerful push from his legs, he leaps into space.

After the diver makes that leap, he does twists and somersaults in the air. As he tumbles through the air, the diver looks for landmarks around him. This helps him turn his body during flight so he hits the water in the right position.

Some divers make flips or twists on their way down.

A feet-first landing is the safest way to end a dive.

For the diver's safety, the most important part of cliff diving is the water entry. The higher the jump, the faster and more dangerous it is to hit the water. If he dives from 20 feet (6 m), he will hit the water at 25 miles per hour (40 kph). If he dives from 50 feet (15 m), he will reach speeds of 38 miles per hour (61 kph). Divers need to enter the water feet first, pointing their bodies like a pencil. His arms should be at his side, and his feet together pointing downward. Entering the water any other way could cause major injury. If a diver hits the water with his body sideways, like a pancake or a belly-flop, it would be like landing on concrete. A diver who enters the water wrong can break bones or be seriously injured.

Because of this possibility, cliff diving is one of the world's most dangerous sports. Here are three rules cliff divers always follow:

1. Practice low first. Cliff divers practice from a 10-meter (32 feet) platform into a swimming pool.

2. Check out the water first. Make sure it is deep enough and there are no rocks or other objects hiding under the surface.

3. Never dive alone. Even at world-class events, scuba divers are in the water to make sure divers are okay once they splash down.

The boats and divers in the water are ready in case of emergency.

CHAPTER THREE

The Best from On High

Though people have been cliff diving for almost 300 years, it only became a **competitive** sport on March 9, 1968. ABC Sports televised the first International Cliff Diving Championship from Acapulco. The sport did not become totally organized until February 1996, when the World High Diving Federation was formed in Avegno, Switzerland. The federation helps support and organize events all over the world. Red Bull, an extreme sports **sponsor**, runs a Cliff Diving World Series as well.

At a competition, fans watch from boats and from the sides of the cliff as divers compete. Divers jump from heights of 59 to 88 feet (18 to 27 m).

Perfect form is the key to getting good scores.

Cliff diving rules are similar to those for Olympic high diving. Five international judges watch the dives and score the divers on a scale of 0 to 10. The highest and lowest scores are removed from the total. The three remaining scores are added up. Each dive also has a "degree of difficulty" score. If a diver does five somersaults instead of two, this has a higher difficulty score. The total from the three scores is multiplied by the degree of difficulty score. Competitors do three dives. The scores from each dive are added together. The winner is the diver with the highest combined score.

This beachside jump attracted fans in their boats.

Duque shows off one of his many cliff-diving medals.

Orlando Duque of Colombia is one of the world's best cliff divers. He has won nine world titles and is the only diver to ever receive a perfect score from all the judges at once—all 10's. He lives in Hawaii, where he is surrounded by beautiful places to dive.

The Duke started diving when he was 10. He trained six hours a day. He had hopes to qualify for the 1992 Olympics in Barcelona, Spain, when he was 18. But the Colombian Diving Association could not afford to send him to the Games. He headed off to college instead and began training on the side for a new career as a cliff diver. He is the star of his own movie, *9 Dives*, which **chronicles** his diving life.

Gary Hunt of Great Britain is Duque's biggest rival. He beat out The Duke for the 2010 world title. Hunt is also the only cliff diver to ever try a dive with a running takeoff.

Hunt was a swimmer in his early years, but was drawn to the flips and somersaults at the dive pool. By age 10, he had switched to diving. In 2006, when he was 22, he was invited to participate in a 10-meter diving show. A cliff diver was also in this show and asked if Hunt wanted to try cliff diving, and he started his new life.

Gary Hunt shows off his championship form.

The sun and this diver are heading into the ocean at the same time.

"The sport of cliff diving is so special," Hunt says. "There is no sport this extreme where you don't need any machinery or equipment."

The beautiful locations, the thrill of heights, the terrifying speeds—these are just some of the things that make cliff diving so special. It may not be for everybody to actually do, but it is for everybody to watch in awe!

Glossary

chronicles—tells the story of

colossal—enormous, very big

competitive—performed to decide who is the winner

cove—a narrow opening in a cliff or rock face that lets seawater in

crucial—involving an important decision or result, a critical situation

locals—people who reside in an area

pesos—a type of money used in Mexico

sponsor—a company that provides money to put on a sporting event

tourists—people who are traveling for pleasure

BOOKS

*Bring Your "A" Game: A Young Athlete's
Guide to Mental Toughness*
By Jennifer L. Etnier (2009, The University of North Carolina Press)
Read how important being mentally prepared is for cliff divers.
This book helps young athletes in any sport understand how to get
your mind ready to compete.

Frommer's Portable Acapulco
By Shane Christensen (2009, Frommer's)
With a cliff diver featured on the cover, this book includes information
for tourists traveling to Acapulco and nearby cities in Mexico.

Springboard and Platform Diving
By Ron O'Brien (2003, Human Kinetics)
This book is almost an encyclopedia of diving. The author is one of the
best diving coaches ever. He writes about cliff diving, but most of this
book is about other types of diving.

WEB SITES

For links to learn more about extreme sports: **childsworld.com/links**

Note to Parents, Teachers, and Librarians: We routinely verify our Web
links to make sure they are safe and active sites. So encourage your
readers to check them out!

Index

About the Author

Ellen Labrecque is a freelance writer who lives in Pennsylvania with her husband and two kids. She has jumped off cliffs as high as 20 feet in Hawaii. When not vacationing, she loves writing, running, and covering Extreme sports.